vocal · piano

michael bublé
to be loved

ISBN 978-1-4803-5090-8

HAL•LEONARD®
CORPORATION
7777 W. BLUEMOUND RD. P.O. BOX 13819 MILWAUKEE, WI 53213

For all works contained herein:
Unauthorized copying, arranging, adapting, recording, Internet posting, public performance,
or other distribution of the printed music in this publication is an infringement of copyright.
Infringers are liable under the law.

Visit Hal Leonard Online at
www.halleonard.com

YOU MAKE ME FEEL SO YOUNG

Words by MACK GORDON
Music by JOSEF MYROW

© 1946 (Renewed) WB MUSIC CORP.
All Rights Reserved   Used by Permission

IT'S A BEAUTIFUL DAY

Words and Music by MICHAEL BUBLÉ,
ALAN CHANG and AMY FOSTER

© 2013 WB MUSIC CORP., I'M THE LAST MAN STANDING MUSIC, INC., WARNER-TAMERLANE PUBLISHING CORP., IHAN ZHAN MUSIC and SONGS FROM THE HEATLEY CLIFF
All Rights for I'M THE LAST MAN STANDING MUSIC, INC. Administered by WB MUSIC CORP.
All Rights for IHAN ZHAN MUSIC Administered by WARNER-TAMERLANE PUBLISHING CORP.
All Rights for SONGS FROM THE HEATLEY CLIFF Administered by SONGS OF KOBALT MUSIC PUBLISHING
All Rights Reserved   Used by Permission

TO LOVE SOMEBODY

Words and Music by BARRY GIBB
and ROBIN GIBB

Copyright © 1967 by Universal Music Publishing International MGB Ltd., Warner-Tamerlane Publishing Corp. and Crompton Songs LLC
Copyright Renewed
All Rights for Universal Music Publishing International MGB Ltd. in the U.S. and Canada Administered by Universal Music - Careers
International Copyright Secured   All Rights Reserved

bod - y　　　the way＿ I love you.

In my brain＿＿＿＿

I see your face a-gain,　　and I know my＿ frame＿

＿ of mind.＿＿＿＿＿＿＿　You ain't got-ta be so

you don't know ____ what it's like, _____ y - yeah, _____

you don't know ____ what it's like. _____ Y - yeah, _____

you don't know ____ what it's like. __ Ba - by,

you don't know ____ what it's like _____ to love some -

WHO'S LOVIN' YOU

Words and Music by
WILLIAM "SMOKEY" ROBINSON, JR.

© 1960 (Renewed 1988) JOBETE MUSIC CO., INC.
All Rights Controlled and Administered by EMI APRIL MUSIC INC.
All Right Reserved   International Copyright Secured   Used by Permission

since you're gone is cry. _____ Mm, mm,

whoa, _____ mm, whoa, _____ ba - by,

and don't you ev - er won - der

with your pret - ty lit - tle head a - bout what I will

SOMETHING STUPID

Words and Music by
C. CARSON PARKS

Moderately

I know I stand in line __ un-til __ you think you have the time __ to spend an eve-ning with me. __ And if we go some-place to dance, __ I

© Copyright 1967 by Greenwood Music Co., P.O. Box 150202, Nashville, TN 37215 for U.S.A. and Canada
Copyright Renewed
Reproduced by Permission of Montclare Music Co. Ltd., London, England for the British Empire and Commonwealth of Nations (excluding Canada and Australia) and Continent of Europe
International Copyright Secured   All Rights Reserved

love you." ___ I can

see it in your eyes ___ that you de - spise the same old lies ___ you heard the

night be - fore; ___ and

though it's just a line ___ to you, ___ for me it's true, ___ and it nev - er seemed ___ so

COME DANCE WITH ME

Words by SAMMY CAHN
Music by JAMES VAN HEUSEN

Copyright © 1959 Cahn Music Co. and Maraville Music Corp.
Copyright Renewed
Worldwide Rights for Cahn Music Co. Administered by Imagem Sounds
International Copyright Secured   All Rights Reserved

CLOSE YOUR EYES

Words and Music by MICHAEL BUBLÉ,
ALAN CHANG and JANN ARDEN RICHARDS

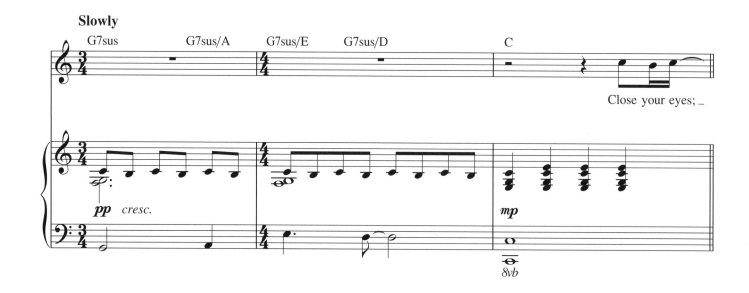

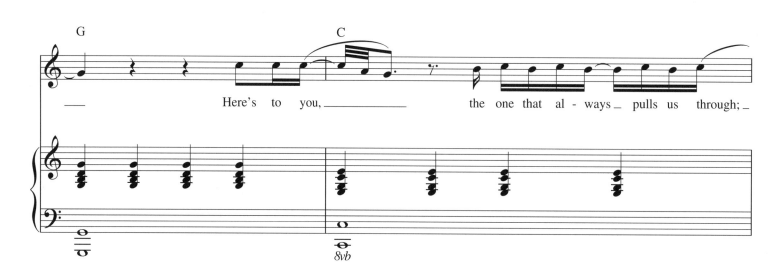

© 2013 WB MUSIC CORP., I'M THE LAST MAN STANDING MUSIC, INC., WARNER-TAMERLANE PUBLISHING CORP.,
IHAN ZHAN MUSIC, UNIVERSAL MUSIC PUBLISHING CANADA and GIRL ON THE MOON MUSIC II
All Rights for I'M THE LAST MAN STANDING MUSIC, INC. Administered by WB MUSIC CORP.
All Rights for IHAN ZHAN MUSIC Administered by WARNER-TAMERLANE PUBLISHING CORP.
All Rights for UNIVERSAL MUSIC PUBLISHING CANADA and GIRL ON THE MOON MUSIC II in the U.S. and Canada Controlled and Administered by
UNIVERSAL - POLYGRAM INTERNATIONAL PUBLISHING, INC.
All Rights Reserved   Used by Permission

AFTER ALL

Words and Music by MICHAEL BUBLÉ,
ALAN CHANG, STEVEN SATER,
BRYAN ADAMS and JIM VALLANCE

© 2013 WB MUSIC CORP., I'M THE LAST MAN STANDING MUSIC, INC., WARNER-TAMERLANE PUBLISHING CORP.,
IHAN ZHAN MUSIC, KUKUZO MUSIC, BADAMS MUSIC LTD. and VALLANTUNES
All Rights for I'M THE LAST MAN STANDING MUSIC, INC. Administered by WB MUSIC CORP.
All Rights for IHAN ZHAN MUSIC and KUKUZO MUSIC Administered by WARNER-TAMERLANE PUBLISHING CORP.
All Rights for BADAMS MUSIC LTD. Controlled and Administered by EMI APRIL MUSIC INC.
All Rights for VALLANTUNES Controlled and Administered by OLE RED CAPE SONGS
All Rights Reserved   Used by Permission

that you ___ can ___ fall ___ in love with me ___ a - gain, ___
that I ___ can ___ fall ___ in love with you ___ a - gain, ___

and we'll both ___ be stand - ing tall ___ af - ter all. ___
and I'll catch ___ you when ___ you fall

Oh, af - ter all. ___

(Vocal 1st time only)

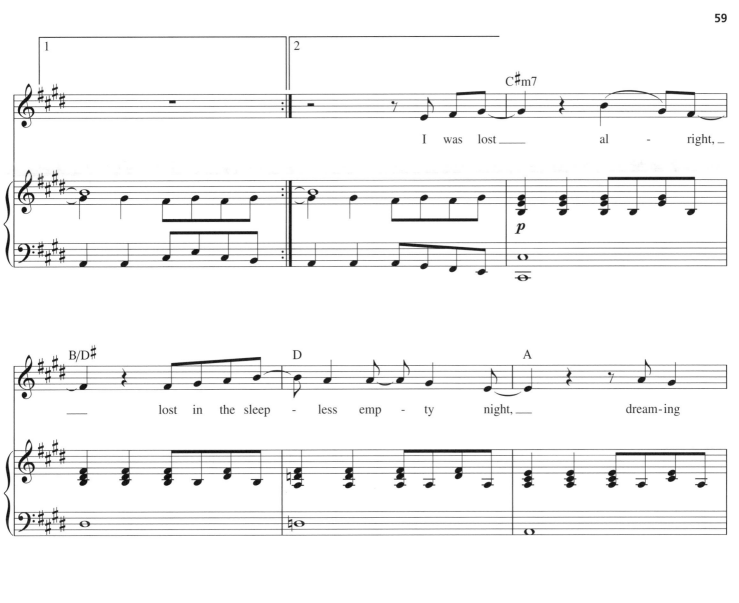

I was lost ___ al - right, ___ lost in the sleep - less emp - ty night, ___ dream-ing

of you; and in those dreams, you still ___ were mine.

D.S. al Coda

Af - ter all, ___

HAVE I TOLD YOU LATELY THAT I LOVE YOU

Words and Music by
SCOTT WISEMAN

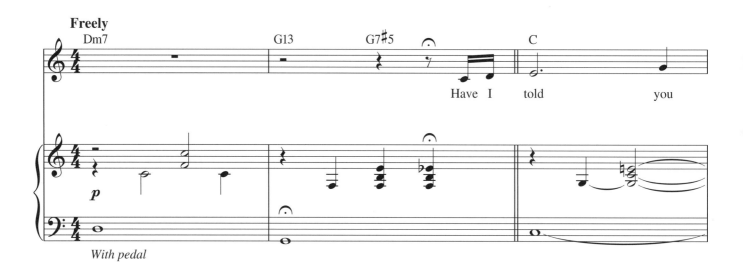

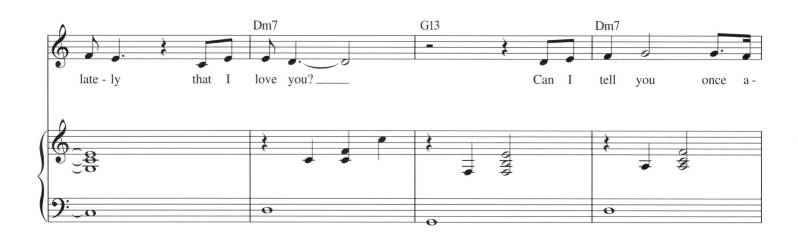

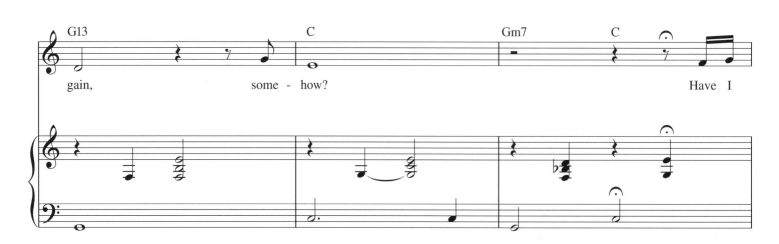

Copyright © 1945, 1946 SONGS OF UNIVERSAL, INC.
Copyrights Renewed
All Rights Reserved   Used by Permission

Have I told you why the nights are long when you're not with me? Well

dar - ling, I'm tell - ing you now.
(Have I told you late - ly, have I told you late - ly, have I told you late - ly,

My heart would break in two if I should
have I told you?)

To Coda ⊕

tell - ing _____ you now. _____
oh my dar - ling, I'm - a, have I told you late - ly?)

Instrumental solo

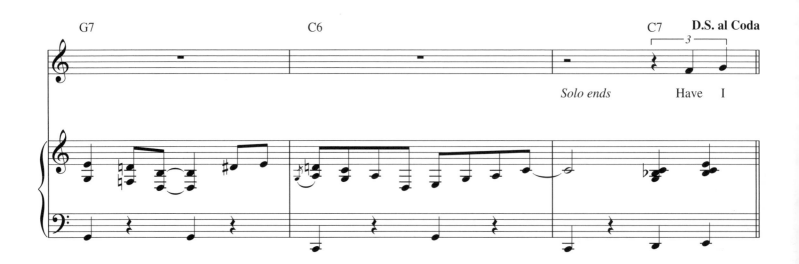

Solo ends   Have I

D.S. al Coda

CODA

TO BE LOVED

Words and Music by BERRY GORDY,
GWEN GORDY FUQUA and TYRAN CARLO

© 1957 (Renewed 1985) JOBETE MUSIC CO., INC., OLD BROMPTON ROAD and THIRD ABOVE MUSIC
All Rights in the U.S. for JOBETE MUSIC CO., INC. and OLD BROMPTON ROAD Controlled and Administered by EMI APRIL MUSIC INC.
All Rights Reserved   International Copyright Secured   Used by Permission

YOU'VE GOT A FRIEND IN ME

from Walt Disney's TOY STORY

Music and Lyrics by
RANDY NEWMAN

© 1995 Walt Disney Music Company
All Rights Reserved   Used by Permission

NEVERTHELESS
(I'm in Love with You)

Words and Music by BERT KALMAR
and HARRY RUBY

Copyright © 1931 by DeSylva, Brown & Henderson, Inc.
Copyright Renewed, Assigned to Chappell & Co. and Harry Ruby Music Co.
All Rights for Harry Ruby Music Co. Administered by The Songwriters Guild Of America
International Copyright Secured   All Rights Reserved

I GOT IT EASY

Words and Music by MICHAEL BUBLÉ,
ALAN CHANG and TOM JACKSON

© 2013 WB MUSIC CORP., I'M THE LAST MAN STANDING MUSIC, INC., WARNER-TAMERLANE PUBLISHING CORP., IHAN ZHAN MUSIC and COSMIC GIGGLE MUSIC
All Rights for I'M THE LAST MAN STANDING MUSIC, INC. Administered by WB MUSIC CORP.
All Rights for IHAN ZHAN MUSIC Administered by WARNER-TAMERLANE PUBLISHING CORP.
All Rights for COSMIC GIGGLE MUSIC Controlled and Administered by IRVING MUSIC, INC.
All Rights Reserved   Used by Permission

bit ___ on this cold _____ rain - y eve - ning; _____

I'm warm ___ in bed, ___ got a beau - ti - ful ___ wom - an be -

neath me ___ ev - 'ry night. _____

I got it eas - y, _____ yeah, _____

YOUNG AT HEART

Words by CAROLYN LEIGH
Music by JOHNNY RICHARDS

© 1954 CHERIO CORP.
© Renewed CHERIO CORP. and JUNE'S TUNES
All Rights Reserved